Instructor's Manual and Test Bank

to accompany

Leisure and Life Satisfaction
Foundational Perspectives

Third Edition

Christopher R. Edginton
University of Northern Iowa

Debra J. Jordan
Oklahoma State University

Donald G. DeGraaf
Calvin College

Susan R. Edginton
University of Northern Iowa

Boston   Burr Ridge, IL   Dubuque, IA   Madison, WI   New York   San Francisco   St. Louis
Bangkok   Bogotá   Caracas   Kuala Lumpur   Lisbon   London   Madrid   Mexico City
Milan   Montreal   New Delhi   Santiago   Seoul   Singapore   Sydney   Taipei   Toronto

McGraw-Hill Higher Education

A Division of The McGraw-Hill Companies

Instructor's Manual and Test Bank to accompany
LEISURE AND LIFE SATISFACTION: FOUNDATIONAL PERSPECTIVES, THIRD EDITION
CHRISTOPHER R. EDGINTON, DEBRA J. JORDAN, DONALD G. DEGRAAF, SUSAN R. EDGINTON

1 2 3 4 5 6 7 8 9 0 QPD QPD 0 3 2

ISBN 0-07-235398-8

www.mhhe.com

Contents

Introduction

This Instructor's Manual and Test Bank was developed for use with *Leisure and Life Satisfaction: Foundational Perspectives,* Third Edition. It is organized to include two basic sections. First is an outline of discussion topics that can be used to guide class lectures and other activities. Second is the Test Bank, which includes three types of questions for each chapter. The basic concept of each chapter is addressed in both sections.

Organization of Textbook

The gift of leisure in its fullness is about promoting human happiness and satisfaction. The work of leisure professionals is to improve and enhance the human condition. Such individuals create a sense of hope, underscoring the promise of greater life satisfaction through leisure. The underlying theme of *Leisure and Life Satisfaction* suggests that leisure is a powerful vehicle that is available to individuals to assist them in achieving these ends. The role of professionals is one of crafting leisure environments to assist individuals, groups of people, and whole communities in achieving a higher quality of life and a greater lever of happiness and satisfaction.

Leisure and Life Satisfaction was conceptualized as an introductory textbook. The intent was to address introductory classes dealing with recreation, parks, or leisure services. Organized in three major sections, the book provides a comprehensive overview of the phenomenon of leisure in North American society, the delivery of leisure services, and critical and relevant issues impacting professional practice. The first section focuses on a basic understanding of the phenomenon of leisure in North American society. We wanted to provide information that is conceptually, philosophically, historically, and sociologically based to help students understand the value and importance of leisure in our society. It was important to address leisure throughout the entire lifespan as a part of this initial section of the book. The second section of the book highlights how leisure services are organized and implemented in North American society in all sectors. We addressed the organization of services at the local, state, and federal government levels as well as the provision of services in non-governmental organizations and the commercial sectors. Following the first edition of the book, a chapter on therapeutic recreation was added because of the large number of individuals involved in providing services for disabled persons. This chapter remains in the third edition. The last section of the book deals with issues related to professional practice. In particular, we were interested in assisting students in their career development as well as addressing such salient issues as diversity, programming concerns (the heart of the work of leisure service professionals), and future perspectives. This section also provides information regarding work with professional organizations and societies.

The third edition of *Leisure and Life Satisfaction*, like its predecessor, provides a complete overview of many of the aspects of leisure, including basic concepts, definitions, fundamentals, and terms; the organization and delivery of leisure services; and critical professional trends, issues, and future perspectives. It was important for us to include key statistics and information regarding leisure and the profession to provide depth and breadth to the work rather than offering only a surface treatment of the information. We were interested in providing a document that was scholarly yet user-friendly. *Leisure and Life Satisfaction* was written to assist individuals, especially those preparing themselves to serve as entry-level 5 professionals, to understand the broad dimensions of the leisure phenomenon in North American society, the organization of the leisure industry in all sectors, and issues influencing professional practice. In addition, the third edition of *Leisure and Life Satisfaction* provides up-to-date facts, statistics, and support materials. The text is written with a North American perspective to include examples from both Canada and the United States. Each chapter is enhanced with complementary features, called *Leisure Lines*. These exhibits illustrate key concepts as well as elements related to professional practice.

We also emphasize the idea of life satisfaction as a central integrating theme for our professional work. This concept is not a part of other introductory textbooks, although it is frequently referenced in the literature when discussions of leisure emerge. We also felt that we had been able to incorporate an unusual amount of information from allied professions and other areas of study. We believe that this provides a more holistic treatment of the subject matter and strengthens the presentation.

Well-documented, *Leisure and Life Satisfaction* was written to include several key features as follows:
- Incorporates into one introductory textbook information concerning the leisure phenomenon, delivery of leisure services, and issues impacting on professional practice.
- Provides up-to-date key information, with great depth to the analysis.
- Highlights numerous examples from current professional practice and the leisure lives of individuals.
- Addresses conceptual, historical, philosophical, and social/psychological perspectives of leisure as well as professional concerns.
- Incorporates the concept of life satisfaction as a central integrating theme.
- Effectively incorporates diversity.
- Provides interesting and insightful exhibits, known as *Leisure Lines* (complementing or highlighting key factors), to stimulate discussion among students.
- Offers a thorough discussion related to career development as a teaching method for students. Includes discussion of developing a portfolio.
- Provides great insight into leisure throughout the life cycle.
- Helps the reader understand the existence of mass leisure in contemporary society.
- Provides the reader with insightful information regarding future trends and issues in a broader context. The presentation leaves open the possibility for extended discussions between professor and students.
- Uses figures to illustrate the basic concepts in order to help students gain a broad understanding of the field.

Organization of Instructor's Manual and Test Bank

The Instructor's Manual and Test Bank to accompany *Leisure and Life Satisfaction* is organized by chapter. We have included an outline for discussion for each of the chapters of the book. In general, this outline follows the major headings found within each chapter, although additional material from the text has been incorporated to enhance these outlines. The outlines may also be combined into a course outline and used to provide information for students as a guideline for topics to be covered in individual class sessions. The second section of the book focuses on the creation of test questions. We have developed multiple types of test questions, including essay, multiple choice, and true/false, with 30 different questions for every chapter. The essay questions may also be useful as discussion items in class. We have framed the Test Bank in this way to provide varying approaches to evaluation. The test questions are suggested ones as they have not been validated or reliability-tested. We would encourage you to share with us materials that you have developed so that we may incorporate them in future editions of the Instructor's Manual and Test Bank for *Leisure and Life Satisfaction*.

Acknowledgments

The authors would like to acknowledge the work of Lynda Moore. Lynda's tireless effort and energy were essential in providing clerical assistance and support to this project. We thank her for her effort.

CHAPTER 1
Leisure and Life Satisfaction

CONCEPT: Leisure and life satisfaction are related to one another in today's society.

Outline of Discussion

I.   Leisure toward the 21st century
    A.   We are in the life satisfaction business.
    B.   Generational perspectives of leisure
II.   Life satisfaction
    A.   Defining life satisfaction
    B.   Leisure and its relationship to life satisfaction
    C.   Leisure and life satisfaction as related to age
    D.   Work, leisure, and life satisfaction
    E.   Leisure, satisfaction, and community well-being
III.   Lifestyle management and leisure
    A.   Lifestyle management
    B.   Leisure, organizations, and life satisfaction
IV.   What motivates people to pursue leisure?
    A.   Leisure motives
V.   Constraints to leisure
    A.   Defining constraints
    B.   Antecedent constraints
    C.   Intervening constraints
    D.   Why study constraints?

CHAPTER 2
The World of Leisure, Recreation, and Play

CONCEPT: Defining leisure, recreation and play from a number of perspectives.

Outline of Discussion

I.   The task of defining leisure
        A.   Defining leisure, recreation and play.
        B.   Defining and measuring leisure, recreation and play: Key to predicting consequences of actions as professionals.
II.   What is Leisure?
        A.   Classical definitions
        B.   Factors Related to a Satisfying Leisure Experience
                1.   Perceived freedom
                2.   Perceived competence
                3.   Intrinsic motivation
                4.   Positive affect
        C.   Ways of Viewing Leisure
                1.   Leisure as time
                2.   Leisure as activity
                3.   Leisure as state of mind
                4.   Leisure as a symbol of social status
                5.   Leisure as a social instrument
                6.   Leisure as a anti-utilitarian concept
                7.   Leisure as a holistic concept
        D.   Serious Leisure
        E.   Work and leisure
                1.   What is work
                2.   What is the relationship between work and leisure
                3.   Neulinger's Model of Leisure
III.   What is recreation
        A.   Classical definitions
        B.   Common elements of definitions of recreation
        C.   Recreation as a social instrument
IV.   What is play?
        A.   Classical definitions
        B.   Theories of play
                1.   Surplus energy theory
                2.   Recreation theory
                3.   Pre-exercise theory
                4.   Recapitulation theory
                5.   Relaxation theory
                6.   Catharsis theory
                7.   Compensatory theory
                8.   Psychoanalytic theory
                9.   Developmental theory
                10.   Generalization theory
                11.   Attribution theory
                12.   Achievement-motivation theory
                13.   Optimal arousal theory

3

14. Autotelic or flow experience theory
15. Conflict-enculturation theory
C. Common elements in defining play

CHAPTER 3
Leisure: A Historical Perspective

CONCEPT: Knowledge of the history of leisure in pre-literate, agricultural, industrial and contemporary times is important in understanding the movement.

Outline of Discussion

I. What is history
    A. A definition of history
    B. What is historical research
II. Why do we study history
    A. Knowledge of leisure concepts
    B. Appreciation for the foundations of the profession
    C. Understanding people in history
    D. Knowledge of significant historical events and places
    E. Knowledge that can be useful—present and future
    F. Understanding our place in history
III. The history of leisure
    A. Leisure in preliterate societies
        1. Survival is the main concern for life
        2. Difficult to distinguish between work and play
        3. Individuals live by natural life rhythms
    B. Leisure in the agricultural era
        1. The first form of culture was agriculture
        2. Properties rights created division of labor, leisure class emerges
        3. Individuals were regulated by the seasons
        4. Leisure in ancient Greece
        5. Leisure in ancient Rome
        6. Leisure and Christianity
    C. Industrial revolution in Leisure
        1. Class distinctions were sharpened between men and women
        2. Life became clock driven
        3. Urbanization, child labor and industrialization resulted in the need for social reform.
        4. Movements and institutions
        5. The rise of municipal parks
        6. The rise of national parks
        7. The rise of state parks
        8. The play movement
        9. Establishment of youth-serving and volunteering organizations
        10. The power of passion
        11. The evolving nature of programs
        12. Inclusivity
IV. The technological or information era
    A. Information era results in massive changes to the society as computers and the nature of work changes the basic socioeconomic structure.
    B. Factors that impact on Leisure, Youth & Human Services
        1. Cultural pluralism
        2. Urban versus rural society
        3. Human resources

4. New technology
5. Changing demographics
6. Movement from institutional help to self-help
7. Spiritual and personal fulfillment
8. Sophisticated communication
9. Rapid mobility
C. Changes in perceptions of leisure
    1. Environmental services
    2. Services for people with difficulties
    3. Travel and tourism
    4. Commercial leisure services

CHAPTER 4
Philosophical and Conceptual Themes

CONCEPT: Developing a philosophy to guide one's professional actions and understanding of the relationship between philosophy, values and ethics.

Outline of Discussion

I.   Why philosophy?
      A.   Philosophy of leisure is useful in guiding the work of the profession.
      B.   A philosophy of leisure helps one understand the "whys" of professional action
II.   What is philosophy?
      A.   Philosophy is a collection of systematically defined values, beliefs and preferences
      B.   Philosophy and circumstances – from where do philosophical ideas come?
      C.   Searching for a philosophical attitude.
            1.   Leisure as a means for pursuing divine ends
            2.   Happiness
            3.   Combination of work, play, love an worship
            4.   Self-actualization
            5.   Play
            6.   No final end
            7.   Others
      D.   Values of philosophy
            1.   Preservation of natural resources
            2.   Conservation of natural resources
            3.   Wise use of leisure
            4.   Democracy, citizenship, freedom of choice
            5.   Human happiness
            6.   Protection and promotion of human dignity
            7.   Personal growth
            8.   Leisure awareness
            9.   Leadership and moral character development
            10.   Quality of Life
III.   Values and Ethics
      A.   A value free environment
      B.   Values shape individual lives
      C.   The need for clarity
      D.   The good life
      E.   Values as underlying structures
      F.   The value in an ethic of care
IV.   Why Build a Philosophy of Leisure?
      A.   To know yourself and your organization
      B.   To clarify relationships with consumer/clients
      C.   To clarify relationships within the organization
      D.   To clarify relationships with other institutions
V.   Major Philosophies
      A.   Perennialism
      B.   Idealism
      C.   Realism
      D.   Pragmatism
      E.   Experimentalism

      F.   Existentialism

      G.   Humanism

VI.   Considerations of building a philosophy

      A.   Examine the historical philosophical foundations of the profession

      B.   Examine one's own personal values

      C.   Discuss with professionals their philosophy and values

      D.   Examine the values of organizations delivering leisure services

      E.   Examine the values of the local community

      F.   Examine the values of society as a whole as they relate to leisure.

VII.   The meaning of a philosophy is foundation upon which it builds its services

      A.   An organization's philosophy is foundation upon which it builds its services

      B.   An organization's philosophy results in the creation of a culture which reflects its norms, customs and values

CHAPTER 5
Mass Leisure

CONCEPT: The phenomenon of mass leisure is explored in order to help students understand how it shapes and reflects culture.

Outline of Discussion

I.   Mass Leisure
      A.   Mass leisure is similar to mass culture
      B.   Mass leisure has grown tremendously in the last century
      C.   Canadians and U.S. citizens are moving toward becoming a leisure democracy
II.   Mass Leisure: Is there time?
      A.   Debate as to whether U.S. citizens and Canadians have "run out of time"
      B.   Time famine
      C.   View of time has changed
      D.   A focus of experiences
      E.   Possible future views of time
III.   Mass Leisure: common elements
      A.   Increase in Discretionary Income
      B.   Change in Values
      C.   Improved Infrastructure Related to Physical and Natural Resources
      D.   Improved Technology
IV.   Mass Leisure: What Do People Do?
      A.   Social Activities as Mass Leisure
            1.   Building the social capital needed for leisure and life
            2.   Social activities
            3.   Social leisure: value laden or value free
      B.   Sport as Mass Leisure
      C.   Cultural Activities as Mass Leisure
      D.   The Environment and Mass Leisure
      E.   Tourism as Mass Leisure
      F.   Mass Media and Leisure
            1.   Television viewing as mass leisure
            2.   Movies and mass leisure
            3.   Other forms of media and mass media

CHAPTER 6
Leisure and Life Cycle

CONCEPT: Human development and its relationship to leisure is explored with an emphasis on life stages and leisure lifestyles.

Outline of Discussion

I.   Leisure throughout the Life Cycle
II. Lifestyles
    A. The strugglers
    B. The anxious
    C. The enthusiasts
    D. The self-reliants
    E. Today traditionalists
III. The Life Cycle
IV. Stages of Human Development—Erickson's life stages
    A. Infancy
    B. Young childhood
    C. Middle childhood
    D. Late childhood
    E. Adolescence
    F. Young adulthood
    G. Middle adulthood
    H. Old age
V.   Childhood and Leisure
    A. Midget gurus of play
    B. Periods of childhood
        1. Infancy and toddlers (birth to three)
        2. Pre-school children (4-5 year olds)
        3. Younger children (6-8 year olds)
        4. Older children (9-12 year olds)
    C. The role of youth sports in leisure lives of children
    D. Serving children: Implications for leisure service programs
VI. Adolescence and leisure
    A. 10 basic needs of youth
        1. A need for positive social interaction
        2. A need for safety, structure and clear limits
        3. A need for belonging and meaningful involvement in family, school, community
        4. A need for creative expression
        5. A need for feeling self-worth/giving to others
        6. A need for physical activity
        7. A need to feel a sense of independence, autonomy and control
        8. A need for closeness in relationships
        9. A need for feeling a sense of competence and achievement
        10. A need for a sense of individualism, identity and self-definition
    B. Youth development competencies
        1. Health/physical competence
        2. Personal/social competence
        3. Cognitive/creative competence

  4. Vocational competence

  5. Citizenship competencies

VII. Adulthood and Leisure

 A. Periods of adulthood

  1. Early childhood

   a. Issues of early adulthood – intimacy and establishment of family

   b. Leisure activities – lifelong sports

    2. Middle adulthood

     a. Issues of middle adulthood – establishment of career, stability, security and control

     b. Leisure activities – lifelong sports

   3. Late adulthood

     a. Issues of middle adulthood – career, stability, security and control

     b. Basic functions of leisure activities

 B. Implications for leisure service organizations

   1. Programs for self-directed leisure

   2. Program to promote lifelong leisure

   3. Variety of programs need to offered in innovative ways

VIII. Older Adults and Leisure

 A. Characteristics of older Americans

 B. Stereotypes of the elderly

 C. Two types of elderly in relation to leisure participation

   1. Expanders

   2. Contractors

 D. Age: The "false" variable of leisure behavior

 E. Theories of leisure participation of the elderly

   1. Activity theory

   2. Disengagement theory

 F. Leisure and the elderly: Implications for leisure services organizations

   1. Choice

   2. Participant involvement

   3. Integrated rather than segregated activities

   4. Innovation

   5. Sensitivity

CHAPTER 7
Delivery of Leisure Services: Local Government

CONCEPT: An awareness of public leisure services delivered by local government is explored.

Outline of Discussion

I. Local government and leisure
   A. Local government services are those that are provided at the subdivision of government, which is the closet to the customer
   B. Park and recreation services are provided by nearly every community across the United States and Canada as a part of local services

II. Characteristics of local leisure service agencies
   A. Goals and functions
   B. Research base
   C. Characteristics of professionals
   D. Orientation to customers

III. Types of local leisure service agencies
   A. Statutory laws supporting the provision of local 0ark and recreation services
   B. Municipal government
   C. County government
   D. Special districts
   E. Recreation services as part of a school district

IV. Types of Services
   A. Recreation activity
   B. Areas and facilities
   C. Information
   D. Leadership

V. Professional role and opportunities
   A. District service roles
   B. Supervisory roles
   C. Administrative roles

VI. Career opportunities in public parks and recreation

VII. Challenges for the future
   A. Marketing orientation
   B. Fees and charges
   C. Quality services
   D. Building partnerships
   E. Contracting services
   F. Networking
   G. Diversity
   H. Inclusion
   I. Child care
   J. Youth development
   K. Developing social capitol
   L. Open space
   M. New urbanism
   N. Documenting benefits

CHAPTER 8
Delivery of Leisure Services: State Government

CONCEPT: Goals and functions of state/provincial government in providing leisure experiences reviewed.

Outline of Discussion

I. State government and leisure
   A. Tenth amendment of the constitution: The states' rights amendment
   B. Increasing involvement in providing recreation facilities and programs
II. Characteristics of local leisure service agencies
   A. Goals and Functions
      1. Legislation
      2. Creation of standards and certifications
   B. Coordination with federal and local government
   C. Financial resource base
      1. Taxes
      2. Fees and charges
      3. Federal funds
      4. Endowments and trusts
      5. Sales revenue from concessions and retail outlets
   D. Characteristics of professionals
III. Direct recreation facilities, resources and services provided by states/provinces
   A. Outdoor recreation and resources
      1. State/provincial parks
      2. State/provincial forests
      3. State/provincial fish and wildlife agencies
   B. Tourism promotion
      1. Economic impact of tourism
      2. The "war" to entice visitors
VIII. The arts
   A. State/provincial art agencies
   B. The enabling role of state/provincial art agencies
   C. Strategies for strengthening state/provincial art programs
IX. Other state services
   A. Correctional institutions
   B. State/provincial hospitals and institutions
   C. Car and activity centers
   D. Substance abuse and chemical dependency rehabilitation programs
   E. Museums
   F. Fairgrounds
   G. Cultural programs and facilities
X. Challenges for the future
   A. Changing funding appropriations
   B. Cutbacks in budgets
   C. Public/private partnership
   D. Fees and charges

CHAPTER 9
Delivery of Leisure Services: Federal Government

CONCEPT: An awareness of leisure services delivered by federal government.

Outline of Discussion

I.   Federal government and leisure
II.   Characteristics of federal leisure Service agencies
      A.   Goals and functions
      B.   Resource base
      C.   Characteristics of professionals
      D.   Customer orientation
III.   Types of federal agencies: United States
      A.   U.S. Forest Service
      B.   Bureau of Land Management
      C.   National Park Service
      D.   U.S. Forest Service
      E.   U.S. Fish and Wildlife Service
      F.   Bureau of Indian Affairs
      G.   U.S. Corps of Engineers
      H.   Tennessee Valley Authority
      I.   Bureau of Reclamation
      J.   Veteran's Administration
      K.   Morale, Welfare, and Recreation Services, U.S. Armed Forces
      L.   National Endowment for the Arts
      M.   National Endowment for the Humanities
IV   Types of federal agencies: Canada
      A.   Sports Canada
      B.   Parks Canada
      C.   Health Canada
      D.   Canadian Tourism Commission
IV.   Challenges for the future
      A.   Decrease of funding
      B.   Continuation of the land and water conservation fund act
      C.   Competition over use of resources
      D.   Lack of consistency in the political environment
      E.   Consumptive versus non-consumptive pursuits

CHAPTER 10
Delivery of Leisure Services: Non-Profit

CONCEPT: Non-profit organizations and leisure services are the key concepts explored in this chapter.

Outline of Discussion

I.   Non-profit organizations and leisure
      A.   Non-profit organizations involve large numbers of volunteers
      B.   Altruistic volunteerism is an important trait among U.S. citizens and Canadians. We are a nation of joiners

II.   Characteristics of Private, Non-profit Leisure Service Organizations
      A.   Goals and functions
      B.   Resource base
      C.   Fundraising
      D.   Partnerships and building collaborative relationships

III.   Characteristics of professionals
      A.   Range of personnel

IV.   Types of youth and voluntary non-profit leisure service organizations
      A.   Youth serving organizations
      B.   Non-sectarian sponsored organizations
            1.   4-H Youth for America
            2.   Boy Scouts of America
            3.   Girl Scouts of the U.S.A.
            4.   Junior Achievement
            5.   Camp Fire Girls and Boys, Inc.
            6.   Girls, Inc.
            7.   Boys and Girls Clubs of America
            8.   Big Brother/Big Sisters of American
      C.   Religiously organizations
      D.   Religious organizations
      E.   Organizations serving special populations
            1.   USO
            2.   Recreation Center for Handicapped, INC
            3.   Eckerd Foundation
      F.   Relief and social service organizations
            1.   American Red Cross
      G.   Social service organizations
            1.   Metropolitan Family Service
      H.   Conservation organizations
            1.   Sierra Club
      I.   Service Clubs

V.   Challenges for the future
      A.   Expanding services to younger children
      B.   Fundraising
      C.   Volunteer workers
      D.   Staff development
      E.   Developing partnerships

CHAPTER 11
Delivery of Leisure Services: Commercial

CONCEPT: An awareness of leisure services delivered by commercial organizations is the focus of this area.

Outline of Discussion

I.   Commercial organizations in leisure
    A.   Nearly 90 percent of all expenditures for leisure are in the commercial
    B.   Professionals in this area care about quality of service as well as producing a profit for their effort
II.   Characteristics of commercial leisure services
    A.   Goals and functions
    B.   Resource base
    C.   Characteristics of professional/owners
    D.   Orientation to customers
III.   Types of business ownership
    A.   Sole proprietorship
    B.   Partnerships
    C.   Corporations
IV.   Types of commercial leisure services
    A.   Travel and tourism
    B.   Hospitality and food service
        1.   Resorts
        2.   Hostels
        3.   Hotel
        4.   Motels
        5.   Restaurants
        6.   Bed and breakfast inns
        7.   Convention centers
        8.   Casinos and resorts
    C.   Leisure products (manufacturing)
    D.   Entertainment services
        1.   Professional sports
        2.   Gaming establishment
        3.   Horse racing and dog racing
        4.   Automobile racing
        5.   Circuses and carnivals
        6.   Theme and amusement parks
        7.   Special events and festivals
        8.   Live, filmed, taped or broadcast performance
    E.   Retail outlets
        1.   Specialty stores
        2.   Variety stores
        3.   Department stores
        4.   Full line discount store
        5.   Retail catalog storeroom
        6.   Factory outlet
        7.   Flea market

8.   Video ordering store
F.   Leisure Services in the Natural Environment
     1.   Land based
     2.   Water based
     3.   Air based
     4.   Historically and cultural based
     5.   Geographically based

V.   Entrepreneurship, opportunities, and challenges
A.   What is entrepreneurship?
B.   Opportunities in the commercial leisure service sector
     1.   Prospects for profits
     2.   The top leisure industries
     3.   Small leisure businesses
C.   Challenges to the entrepreneur
     1.   Changing conditions
     2.   Capital
     3.   Seasonal factors
     4.   Ethical considerations
     5.   Risk management
     6.   Social responsibilities
     7.   Consumer protection
     8.   Knowledge of customers
     9.   Lack of personal time
     10.   Inadequate managerial programs
     11.   Over-regulations

CHAPTER 12
Delivery of Leisure Services: Therapeutic Recreation

CONCEPT: Therapeutic recreation and inclusive recreation programs are reviewed.

Outline of Discussion

I.   Therapeutic recreation services
    A.   Therapeutic recreation services
    B.   Special recreation
    C.   The right thing to do
II. The emergence of therapeutic recreation as a profession
    A.   The Need for specialized services
    B.   The Influx of wounded soldiers from the world wars
    C.   Professional organizations
    D.   Legislation
III. Characteristics of therapeutic recreation: people with disabilities today
    A.   People with disabilities today
    B.   Barriers to success in leisure
    C.   Goals and functions
    D.   Resource base
    E.   Characteristics of Professionals
IV. Types of therapeutic recreation programs/settings
    A.   Outpatient clinics
    B.   Group homes
    C.   Home health care agencies
    D.   Substance abuse facilities
    E.   Halfway houses
    F.   Vocational training centers
    G.   Camps
    H.   Centers for independent living
    I.   Sheltered workshops
    J.   Community mental health centers
    K.   Adult day care centers
    L.   Senior centers
    M.   Psychiatric facilities
    N.   Hospitals
    O.   Nursing homes
    P.   Settings serving elderly persons
    Q.   Schools or residential centers for those with specific disabilities
    R.   Penal institutions and other programs for socially deviant persons
    S.   Centers for physical medicine and rehabilitation
    T.   Programs of voluntary agencies
    U.   Public recreation and parks department
V.   Challenges for the future
    A.   Dealing with assistive technology
    B.   Addressing new/growing social problems

CHAPTER 13
Leisure Programming: Promoting Quality Services

CONCEPT: Strategies and methods for planning, organizing, promoting, implementing and evaluating leisure services with an emphasis on providing quality services.

Outline of Discussion

I. Leisure Programming
    A. Greater accountability requires a focus on quality and value
    B. Programs, the products produced by programmers, enable customers to enjoy the benefits or outcomes of leisure experiences
II. Promoting Quality and Value
    A. Quality is a perception of excellence
    B. Value can be thought of as the return on one's investment
    C. Building a commitment to quality
III. Developing a service orientation
    A. What is a service? What is a product?
    B. Organizing a strategy to produce service
    C. Value added services
    D. Positive customer relations
    E. Organizational policies and procedures
IV. Programs: The services of leisure service organizations
    A. Types of programs
        1. Activities
        2. Areas and facilities
        3. Information
        4. Leadership
    B. Factors influencing leisure program planning
        1. Generation
        2. Environmental factors
        3. Level of education
        4. Cultural background
    C. The process of program planning
        1. The development of program goals
        2. Needs assessment
        3. Program planning
        4   Program evaluation
V. Management approaches to programming
    A. Total Quality Program Panning
    B. Just-in-Time Programming
    C. Agile Leisure Programming
    D. Benefits-Based Programming
VI. Roles of leisure programmers
    A. Professionals perform three roles—management, supervisory and direct service
    B. Direct service roles
        1. Direct program leadership
        2. Team leadership
        3. Instructional leadership
        4. Official/referee

5. Host/guide interpreter
6. Counselor
7. Outreach worker
8. Facility operator
9. Sales personnel

CHAPTER 14
Professional Career Development

CONCEPT: Understanding how to pursue a professional career in the leisure service area is the focus of this chapter.

Outline of Discussion

I. Pursuing a professional career
    A. A career in the leisure field can be exciting, dynamic, meaningful, challenging and a valuable work and life experience
    B. Leisure service professionals master a unique body of knowledge that enables them to provide a unique and valuable service to society.
II. Common elements of a profession
    A. An organized body of knowledge
    B. Organizations and institutions that exist to transmit professional knowledge
    C. Creation of professional authority as a result of public sanction
    D. Code of ethics
    E. Commitment to professional ideals
III. Professional associations
    A. Examples of professional associations
        1. American Alliance for Health, Physical Education, Recreation and Dance (AAHPERD)
        2. American Association for Leisure and Recreation (AALR)
        3. American Camping Association (ACA)
        4. Association for Experiential Education (AEE)
        5. American Therapeutic Recreation Association (ATRA)
        6. Canadian Parks/Recreation Association (CPRA)
        7. International Ecotourism Society
        8. International Festivals and Events Association (IFEA)
        9. Employee Services Management Association (ESMA)
        10. National Intramural-Recreation Sports Association (NIRSA)
        11. National Recreation and Park Association (NRPA)
        12. Resort & Commercial Recreation Association (RCRA)
        13. World Leisure and Recreation Association (WLRA)
    B. Special interest groups
    F. Trade associations
    G. Futuristic groups
IV. Pursuing a professional career: Key elements
    A. Career assessment and exploration
    B. Education
    C. Professional experience
    D. Networking
    E. Certifications
    E. Lifelong education and professional development
    F. Use of a professional portfolio

CHAPTER 15
Leisure and Cultural Diversity

CONCEPT: The pursuit of diversity in leisure service experience and organizations is the focus of this chapter.

Outline of Discussion

I.   Future trends: A dramatic increase in diversity
      A.   Basic concepts and definitions
            1.   Culture
            2.   Prejudice
            3.   Discrimination
            4.   Status
      B.   Dimensions of diversity: Within and between group differences
            1.   Primary characteristics
            2.   Secondary characteristics
            3.   Interaction of characteristics
II.   Culture sensitivity: Valuing differences
      A.   A process for valuing differences
III.   Implications of diversity for leisure professionals
      A.   Administrative practices
            1.   Mission statements
            2.   Rules and regulations
            3.   Policies, procedures and practices
            4.   Methods of communication
            5.   Staff development model
            6.   Best organizational practices
      B.   Diversity and leadership
            1.   Direct leadership for diverse groups
            2.   Impact of leader expectations
            3.   Equity issues

CHAPTER 16
Future Trends

CONCEPT: The identification of changing trends in leisure including social, health, environment and technology are included in this chapter.

Outline of Discussion

I. Social trends and leisure
   - A. Shifts in population
   - B. Changes in social roles
   - C. Greater equality in sports and athletics for women
   - D. Blurring of public/private sectors
   - E. Increase in diversity
II. Health trends and issues
   - A. Changes in physical health
   - B. Changes in social health
III. Environmental concerns
   - A. Development versus ecosystems
   - B. Resource depletion
   - C. Environmental degradation
IV. Educational issues
   - A. Desegregation and open enrollment
   - B. Decreased support for extracurricular programs
   - C. Increased emphasis on higher education
V. Technological influences
   - A. Changes in time use
   - B. Systems and innovations in services and equipment
   - C. Transportation
VI. Economic Trends
   - A. Changing nature of work
   - B. Continued growth of the service sector

TEST BANK

CHAPTER 1
Leisure and Life Satisfaction

CONCEPT: Leisure and life satisfaction are related to one another in today's society.

See text p. 6, 9	1.	Describe the importance of leisure and its relationship to life's satisfaction. How does leisure relate to one's quality of life?
See text p. 19	2.	What does the statement mean, "we are in the life satisfaction business?"
See text p. 18, 19	3.	Briefly discuss the motive and benefits of leisure. Create a benefits structure and identify how the use of such a structure can be an aid in one's professional work.
See text p. 23-25	4.	Define and discuss the concept of leisure constraints.
See text p. 3-5	5.	Discuss how generational perspectives influence how we view and participate in leisure.
True	6.	Leisure professionals are in the life satisfaction business
False	7.	Most Canadians and U.S. citizens see play and leisure as being frivolous, nonessential activities or, at best, amusements or diversions.
True	8.	Various generations view leisure and its importance and value differently.
False	9.	The generation that grew up during the Depression has been referred to as the work hard, play hard group
True	10.	Leisure can be defined as a multidimensional construct in which one feels free from constraints, engages in positive affect, is motivated by internal forces and provides an opportunity for perceived competence.
True	11.	Life satisfaction can be defined as a sense of well being, happiness or quality of life that is available to an individual
False	12.	For most individuals, leisure is not an important component contributing to the daily well being of an individual
True	13.	Leisure is a central life force that the individual can shape to have either positive or negative consequences
True	14.	Leisure service organizations play an important role in transmitting the culture of a society.
False	15.	One's attitude toward the use of free time is the greatest barrier to successful leisure participation in activities.
False	16.	Constraints to leisure can be thought of as those factors that do not contribute to the psychological well being of individuals.
False	17.	Most individuals are motivated to use their leisure to seek stimulation.
True	18.	Most leisure activities are noncompulsory, pursued on a voluntary basis or freely chosen
False	19.	Motivation for leisure among women arises primarily from their work commitments
False	20.	Temporal constraints occur when individuals do not have a balance between their leisure and work lives.
False	21.	Americans desire a faster pace of life.
True	22.	Americans are willing to give up pay in order to have more time off.

D   23. The following phrase best captures the current generation's view of leisure.
- A. Leisure and play are frivolous
- B. Leisure is used to restore and refresh oneself
- C. We work to play
- D. Work hard, play hard

C   24. Which of the following elements is not part of Csikszentmihalyi concept of enjoyment or flow?
- A. Merging of action and awareness
- B. Transformation of time
- C. Attitude and character formation
- D. Loss self-conscientiousness

B   25. In promoting life satisfaction, leisure service organizations engage in a number of roles, EXCEPT:
- A Knowledge and skill acquisition
- B. Life generation
- C. Awareness building
- D. Sensory stimulation

D   26. Which is the highest-ranking reason for nonparticipation in leisure services?
- A. Fear of crime
- B. Lack of time
- C. Lack of skill
- D. Site location inconvenient

B   27. The availability of different types of leisure pursuits, including areas and facilities are referred to as
- A. Antecedent constraints
- B. Intervening constraints
- C. Gender constraints
- D. All of the above.

D   28. Which item can be used as criteria for defining happiness or well-being?
- A. External/normative criteria
- B. Internal/subjective criteria
- C. Internal/emotional state
- D. All of the above

D   29. Which of the following can be defined as a leisure motive
- A. Personal development
- B. Therapeutic healing
- C. Freedom and independence
- D. All of the above

C   30. Which of the following is not an identifiable constraint?
- A. Accessibility
- B. Personal reasons
- C. Negative consequences
- D. Time constraints

CHAPTER 2
The World of Leisure, Recreation, and Play

CONCEPT: Defining leisure, recreation and play from a number of perspectives.

See text p. 34	1.	Balancing work and leisure provides time for life. How? What are the challenges?
See text p. 31	2.	What is leisure? Identify and describe how leisure can be defined or viewed.
See text p. 43-44	3.	How is recreation different than leisure?
See text p. 45-46	4.	Identify and define ten theories of play.
See text p. 30-31	5.	How do terms, definitions, and theories assist the leisure service professional in understanding their roles and responsibilities as service providers?
True	6.	In the United Slates and Canada, leisure is usually thought of as free time.
True	7.	The Latin term, *licere,* means to be free.
True	8.	The Greek term, *schole,* can be thought of as a condition of being free from work.
False	9.	Perceived competence refers to the need to exert influence within the context of the leisure experience.
True	10.	When viewing leisure as a state of mind, it can be thought of as being based on an individual's own perspective, feelings, values and past life experiences.
False	11.	The term conspicuous Consumption refers to the consciousness of the individual when he or she is engaged in leisure.
True	12.	The holistic perspective of leisure suggests that ii has potential to be present in many forms of human endeavour.
False	13.	The compensatory theory of leisure suggests that leisure becomes an extension of work.
True	14.	The holistic perspective of leisure provides a fluid, organic approach to defining leisure that may be suited to lifestyles emerging during the information era.
True	15.	Recreation usually is thought of as an activity that is voluntarily and socially redeeming.
True	16.	Play may be defined as a form of human or animal behaviour that is self-motivated and carried on for intrinsic purposes.
True	17.	Serious leisure are those leisure pursuits that require perseverance and special skills.
True	18.	A person who makes homemade furniture during their nonworking hours could be considered a serious leisurist.
True	19.	There is no universally accepted explanation or definition of play.
True	20.	Leisure, recreation, work and play all contribute to one's quality of life.
True	21.	According to Neulinger, a way of viewing the difference between leisure and non-leisure types of experiences is to use the concept of perceived freedom as a primary distinguishing characteristic.
False	22.	When we refer to pure leisure, it is a combination of high-perceived freedom and lower levels of intrinsic motivation.
True	23.	Many theories have emerged to explain play, yet today it has no generally accepted explanation or definition.

B   24. When we are referring to one's perception of the skill level necessary to produce a satisfying experience, we are referring to:
A. Perceived freedom
B. Perceived competence
C. Intrinsic motivation
D. Positive affect

A   25. One of the chief ways of viewing leisure is to break life into three segments—existence, subsistence---existence, subsistence and discretion. This is known as:
A. Time
B. Activity
C. State of Mind
D. Symbol of social status

B   26. Which of the following terms is not used to define leisure.
A. Licere
A. Schole
B. Ascholia
C. School

C   27. The evolution of leisure classes is best reflected in viewing
A. Time
B. Activity
C. State of mind
D. Symbol of social status

D   28. Which of the following elements is <u>not</u> found in most definitions of recreation?
A. Usually results in paid activity
B. Socially redeeming
C. Potential for many desirable outcomes
D. Can be engaged in briefly or in a sustained way

D   29. The joy of playing for its own sake with its own justification is best reflected in the _____ concept of leisure.
A. Time
B. Activity
C. State of mind
D. Social instrument
E. Anti-utilitarian

C   30. Leisure viewed as a useful way of enhancing individual or community life is a reflection of the _____ concept of leisure.
A. Time
B. Activity
C. State of mind
D. Social instrument
E. Anti-utilitarian

CHAPTER 3
Leisure: A Historical Perspective

CONCEPT: Knowledge of the history of leisure in pre-literate, agricultural, industrial and contemporary times are important in understanding the movement.

See text p. 51-52	1.	Define history. Why is it important to understand the history of leisure to be successful as a practicing professional?
See text p. 53, 65-69	2.	It has been written that history is the story about people and their actions and contributions. Pick one historical figure of the park and recreation field and discuss his or her contributions.
See text p. 55	3.	How has the concept of leisure changed from preliterate society to the information era?
See text p. 66-67, 70-71	4.	Explain why the organized park and recreation movement emerged in the United States and Canada around the late 1800s. What were the issues? Why was there a need for social reform and innovation? What parallel's might exist as we move into the 21st century?
See text p.	5.	What projections, based on your knowledge of history, can you make about the evolution of leisure in the 21st century? Will history repeat itself, or will a new dynamic emerge surrounding work and leisure?
True	6.	History is the recording of important events in relationship to an individual concept, person, institution or geographic location.
True	7.	During the industrial revolution, people were tied to a machine, a schedule and a manager in such a way as to compartmentalize their leisure.
False	8.	Leisure pursuits in Roman society were less utilitarian than in Greek society.
True	9.	The Greeks believed that civilization advanced through the cultivation of the mind, body and spirit.
True	10.	The Puritan or Protestant work ethic promotes the desirability of work and thrift.
False	11.	The Lord of Misrule promoted attention to work activities in communities during the Middle Ages
False	12.	During the Renaissance, strict moral codes of the time were maintained in leisure pursuits.
True	13.	During the Industrial Revolution, life became clock-driven, regulating both work and play.
False	14.	The creation of the Commons in New York in 1850 is generally thought to be the first public landscape park in the United States.
False	15.	The founder of landscape architecture in the United States is John Muir.
True	16.	The first state park in the United States was located in Yosemite Valley in California, in 1864.
True	17.	The first national park in the United States was Yellowstone, established in 1872 in the states of Montana, Wyoming and Idaho.
True	18.	The federal Civilian Conservation Corps aided in the development of state park programs in the United States.
True	19.	The Alaska National Interest Lands Conservation Act tripled the size of the national preservation system
False	20.	The Land and Water Conservation Fund Act mandated equal rights for persons with disabilities, including therapeutic recreation services.

True	21.	Entertainment in ancient Rome included gambling, reading, dancing, drinking, and sports.
False	22.	Historians often depict the leisure pursuits of the Greeks as being hedonistic, vulgar, and corrupt.
True	23.	The commercialization of leisure at the turn of the century in America made services more available to the general public.

D   24. Which of the following are reasons for studying the history of the leisure service movement?
   A.   Knowledge of leisure concepts
   B.   Understanding of people, events, and places
   C.   Gaining appreciation for foundations of profession
   D.   All of the above

A   25. Leisure preliterate societies can best be characterized as:
   A.   The integration of life activities
   B.   The separation of work and leisure
   C.   The integration of leisure with harvest activities
   D.   None of the above

D   26. The industrial revolution created the need for programs of social reform primarily because of:
   A.   Child labor
   B.   Urbanization
   C.   Immigration
   D.   All of the above

C   27. Early Christian perspectives of leisure can be differentiated from later perspectives in the following way.
   A.   There is a separation of physical and intellectual labors
   B.   Religious work is superior to other types of work
   C.   Work was good for humankind
   D.   Work and thrift are desirable.

D   28. The municipal park movement in the U.S. began with the establishment of the:
   A.   Boston Commons
   B.   Halifax Commons
   C.   Montreal's Mt. Royal Park
   D.   New York's Central Park

E   29. Jane Addams, a pioneer in leisure services, is best known as
   A.   An environmentalist
   B.   A founder of Hull House
   C.   First president of the American Recreation Society
   D.   Creator of social welfare in America
   E.   B and D

C   30. Luther Gulick and Charlotte Gulick were the co-founders of _____:
   A.   Boy Scouts of America
   B.   Girl Scouts of America
   C.   Camp Fire Girls
   D.   Outward Bound
   E.   All of the above

CHAPTER 4
Philosophical and Conceptual Themes

CONCEPT: Developing a philosophy to guide one's professional actions and understanding of the relationship between philosophy, values and ethics.

See text p. 93-94	1.	Why is a philosophy of leisure important to guiding ones beliefs, values and thoughts related to professional practice?
See text p. 108-109, 111	2.	Identify and discuss the steps in building a philosophy.
See text p. 98-99	3.	Discuss the relationship between values and ethics.
See text p. 102	4.	Discuss your philosophy of leisure (as contrasted with one's professional philosophy)
See text p. 106-108	5.	Identify and discuss from a historical perspective what are some of the values and principles pursued by the park, recreation and leisure service movement.
True	6.	A philosophy of leisure enables professionals to understand the "whys" of their actions.
True	7.	A philosophy is the systematic defining of one's values, beliefs and preferences.
False	8.	A philosophy is usually very concrete and tangible.
False	9.	There has been a good deal of research related to leisure philosophy and ethics.
True	10.	A personal philosophy of leisure can be a source of inspiration and encouragement to an individual.
True	11.	One of the most important uses of one's professional philosophy is to clarify the relationship between customers and professionals.
True	12.	Society tends to view leisure as an end in itself, as conceptually amoral, and focusing on personal expression.
False	13.	The establishment and use of philosophical positions in planning, organizing, and delivering leisure services has been very well used in both Canada and the United States.
True	14.	Humanism has been widely applied to the leisure services field.
True	15.	Professionals working in the field of leisure often develop a well-articulated set of values or philosophies to guide their professional actions.
True	16.	The philosophy of a leisure service organization will be reflected in its culture.
True	17.	The core values of a leisure service organization may focus on such themes as quality consistency, dependability integrity, safety and value.
False	18.	There is a well-developed overarching philosophy guiding the work of leisure service professionals in tile U.S. and Canada to which most individuals are committed.
True	19.	Upon examining philosophical statements of an organization it usually becomes clear that the agency philosophy is based on deeply held agency values.
False	20.	All leisure service agencies share the common value of preservation of the natural environment.
True	21.	It is NOT possible to have a values-free environment.
False	22.	An ethic of care is characterized by assuming that there is one 'right" answer that works for everyone.
True	23.	Policies, procedures program selection, and staffing are all based on an agency's underlying philosophy and ethical position.

D   24. From a historical perspective, the leisure service movement has pursued which of the following values and principles?
              A. Preservation and conservation of natural resources
              B. Wise use of leisure
              C. Human happiness
              D. All of the above

A   25. This philosophy sees leisure as a means to rejuvenate individuals to work more effectively.
              A. Realism
              B. Experimentalism
              C. Existentialism
              D. None of the above

D   26. In building a philosophy, one should
              A. Examine historical foundations of the profession
              B. Examine values of the local community
              C. Examine one's personal values
              D. All of the above

B   27. In terms of philosophy, the majority of writers in the leisure services area have associated values in relationship to
              A. Happiness
              B. Divine ends
              C. Self-actualization
              D. None of the above

B   28. Seeing and responding to needs, a sense of relationship, and dealing with issues while maintaining relationships describes:
              A. Values
              B. Ethic of care
              C. Ethic of rights and justice
              D. Underlying philosophy

G   29. To best develop a personal philosophy of leisure one should:
              A. Talk to professionals in the field
              B. Read books that have a philosophical component to them
              C. Borrow one that already exists
              D. Examine local values
              E. All of the above
              F. Both A and B
              G. A. B. and D

D   30. Achieving fulfillment or self-fulfillment through leisure is referred to as which philosophical approach?
              A. Divine ends
              B. Utopia
              C. Happiness
              D. Self-actualization

CHAPTER 5
Mass Leisure

CONCEPT: The phenomena of mass leisure is explored in order to help students understand how it shapes and reflects culture

See text p. 123-124	1.	What is social capital? Do you think social capital is increasing or decreasing in America today? Explain your answer.
See text p. 116-117, 120	2.	What is mass leisure? List and discuss four of the five reasons we have seen a proliferation of mass leisure in the last century.
See text p. 118	3.	Discuss the idea of time famine. Do you feel it is a problem in this society? Explain. If yes, how should leisure service organizations respond to this phenomenon?
See text p. 130	4.	List and discuss the four major revolutions that have contributed to the proliferation of outdoor recreation in the last 25 years.
See text p. 134-136	5.	How does television impact on society's leisure patterns? What are some of the positive and negative ways that television can impact leisure participation?
False	6.	In the last 10 years the number of hours worked by U.S. citizens has declined by 10%.
True	7.	Leisure mirrors culture and it also shapes culture.
True	8.	In the United States involvement in the "the arts is increasing.
False	9.	Active sports participation is declining as spectator sports continue to grow in popularity.
True	10.	In the 1990s, people took shorter, more frequent vacations.
True	11.	Mass leisure is constantly evolving.
True	12.	For U.S. citizens, more than half of television viewing is done as a secondary activity.
False	13.	Outdoor recreation participation is expected to decrease in the next decade due to the environmental crisis.
True	14.	Canadians and Americans spend more time shopping than any other group of people in the world
False	15.	Home entertainment systems (i.e. VCRs) have led to decreasing attendance at movie theaters.
False	16.	Technology has helped Americans work less and play more.
True	17.	Recent trends suggest that the idea of consuming leisure experiences has increased.
True	18.	Social capital can be viewed as the connections between individuals, networks, norms and trust that enable participants to act together more effectively to pursue shared objectives.
True	19.	Binge drinking is an example of an anti social, negative use of leisure.
False	20.	High culture is "better" than mass culture.
True	21.	Hostelling International's American affiliate is American Youth Hostels who work to fulfill the educational promise of travel.
False	22.	The number of amusement parks in the United States has declined over the last five years.
False	23.	The amount of free time of children and youth is increasing in the United States.

C   24. Leisure democracy refers to:
  A. A place where leisure is an inalienable right
  B. A situation where everyone has the opportunity to give input into what leisure programs will be offered.
  C. A situation where what people do with their free time is determined less by status than by personality and personal interest.
  D. All of the above

D   25. Which of the following social factors have promoted the advancement of mass leisure in this century:
  A. Improved infrastructure
  B. Technology and commercialization of play
  C. Increase in discretionary income
  D. All of the above

D   26. All the following have contributed to the proliferation of outdoor recreation in the 20th century EXCEPT:
  A. Transportation revolution
  B. Equipment revolution
  C. Information revolution
  D. Free time revolution

D   27. Time deepening means:
  A. Undertaking an activity more quickly
  B. Using time more precisely
  C. Understanding more than one activity, simultaneously
  D. All the above.

A   28. Cultural tourism refers to a special form of tourism where:
  A. People choose tourist sites and settings to learn more about local history
  B. The activities must all be done in a natural environment
  C. People are engaged in ecotourism events
  D. None of the above

E   29. Culture is a common thread holding people together. It is affected by
  A. Income
  B. Education levels
  C. Disabilities
  D. Religion
  E. All of the above

B   30. According to Nash the highest use of leisure time is:
  A. Emotional participation
  B. Creative participation
  C. Active participation
  D. Entertainment and amusement

CHAPTER 6
Leisure and the Life Cycle

CONCEPT: Human development and its relationship to leisure is explored with an emphasis on life stages and leisure lifestyles

See text p. 148, 153, 158, 162	1.	Select <u>ONE</u> of the following groups (children, adolescents, adults, or senior citizens) and name two major challenges in providing leisure opportunities to this group.
See text p. 145	2.	Explain why social situation (i.e., married versus single) may be a better indicator of recreation participation than age.
See text p. 161	3.	Discuss the functions of leisure for individuals in late adulthood.
See text p. 157	4.	What are the five basic competencies for youth?
See text p. 143	5.	Briefly discuss some of concerns that leisure service organizations should be aware of in terms of leisure and the lifecycle.
False	6.	The majority of people over 65 reside in institutions for the elderly.
False	7.	Lifetime sports refer to such things as baseball, football and basketball since you can watch them on TV even when bedridden.
True	8.	Adulthood seems to involve several distinct phases.
False	9.	There are more leisure "expanders" than "contractors" in old age
True	10.	During later life and old age leisure becomes increasingly home based with an increased use of public recreation facilities.
False	11.	Lifestyle is the same as lifecycle.
True	12.	The leisure profession should make the growth and development of participants a priority within their organizations and programs.
True	13.	The term lifestyle refers to the person's mode of expression.
True	14.	The holistic perspective of leisure provides a fluid, organic approach to defining leisure that may be suited to lifestyles emerging during the information era.
True	15.	Lifestyles are dynamic and may change during the course of one's lifetime..
False	16.	Play is a learned behavior for children.
False	17.	The period of birth to five years is referred to infancy and toddlerhood.
False	18.	Children in the 1990s have a better level of physical fitness than their counterparts of than 20 years ago.
True	19.	Youth sports programs often exclude youth in high-risk environments (i.e., inner city neighborhoods).
True	20.	Eriksson has identified competency~ a personal identity, and a feeling of closeness or intimacy with others as major issues children must deal with as they develop.
True	21.	Recreational activities during adolescence should be used to promote and maintain autonomy from parents.
False	22.	Children are the most difficult group to serve for public and private, non-profit organizations.
True	23.	Lifelong sports become increasingly important in early to middle adulthood.

C	24.	At what stage in the lifecycle is the desire for novelty the greatest? A. Childhood B. Teen age years C. Adulthood D. Retirement
C	25.	At which age does involvement in competitive sport begin to decline? A. Younger than 6 years of age B. Between 9 and 12 C. Between ages 18 and 21 D. Only after age 55
D	26.	Erickson believe that during older adulthood people experience the conflict between integrity and despair. This means older people A. Are able to generate more money in society B. Are generous with one's knowledge and life C. Understand the links and relationships between generations D. Feel at peace with their contributions to society
A	27.	You have decided to offer programs at your facility to help children improve their social skills, practice fine motor skills, abstract thinking, and emotional impulse control. You are exhibiting and following which perspective of the life cycle? A. Developmental stages B. Ages C. Life events D. None of the above E. All of the above
A	28.	If we followed the life events model of the lifecycle we might offer which of the following? A. Baby changing tables in restrooms B. Cheaper admission prices for children between 10:00 pm and midnight C. Special programs for single people D. Programs that focus on quiet time for older people above E. None of the above
D	29.	Which subgroup of the baby boom generation is the largest? A. The strugglers B. The anxious C. The enthusiasts D. The self-reliants E. Today's traditionalists
E	30.	The 21st century will continue to see A. A blending of recreation activities for those with disabilities and those without disabilities B. Ethnic preferences influencing choice of recreational sports C. An increase in girls involvement in competitive sports D. Active older adults E. All of the above

CHAPTER 7
Delivery of Leisure Services: Local Government

CONCEPT: An awareness of public leisure services delivered by local government is explored.

See text p. 178-179	1.	Identify and discuss the different types of local governmental organizations providing park and recreation services.
See text p. 173-175	2.	List revenue classifications and types used in supporting local park and recreation services.
See text p.179-180	3.	Identify and discuss the five types of legislation that has been created to assist in the establishment of local park and recreation services.
See text p.194-200	4.	Identify and discuss critical issues and trends facing community park and recreation agencies. What agenda might be developed to meet the challenges of today's critical issues?
See text p. 194, 200	5.	What are two of the key trends in society that will impact the park and recreation profession. Explain your answer. What should park and recreation professionals do to address these trends?
False	6.	New Urbanism refers to the growing suburbs around cities today.
True	7.	Municipal parks and recreation programs are offering more integrated programs for persons with disabilities.
False	8.	A youth development approach to programming strives to create a few specific programs in order to build selected skills in participants.
True	9.	The need to build partnerships with the private sector is increasing for municipal park and recreation programs.
True	10.	The future outlook for employment opportunities in local park and recreation systems is good
True	11.	Expenditures for local government for park and recreation services have increased in the past decade.
False	12.	Local parks and recreation departments do not play a key role in the identification and solution of community concerns.
True	13.	In recent years, leisure pools are replacing traditional pools created primarily for exercise and competitive swimming.
True	14.	Single function park and recreation facilities are being replaced with ones built with a multi-use theme.
True	15.	A major challenge to local park and recreation departments has been the expansion o childcare programs.
True	16.	A park and recreation district is an autonomous separate unit of government having a particular purpose.
True	17.	Policy making boards differ from advisory boards in that they have full decision-making power.
False	18.	Regulatory laws refer to those types of laws that empower communities to establish single purpose units of government.
True	19.	Measuring results in government is difficult, as officials focus on inputs such as how many people served rather than qualitative results.
False	20.	Expenditures for local park and recreation department's account for 25% of all local government expenditures.
True	21.	Property taxes account for the largest percentage of all of the revenues collected by local governments.
True	22.	Most local governments receive the majority of their funding from tax dollars.

True   23. Leisure amenities, as reflected in the services provided by a local park and recreation department contributes dramatically to a community's livability.

B   24. This type of legislation is written in a permissive fashion to enable a branch of government to own, operate or manage park and recreation services?
    A. Regulatory law
    B. Enabling law
    C. Special District law
    D. Home rule legislation

D   25. This type of legislation refers to state statutes that provide local subdivisions of government with the ability to determine their own form of organization.
    A. Regulatory law
    B. Enabling law
    C. Special District law
    D. Home rule legislation

D   26. Which of the following is not a service of a county park system?
    A. Regional park and recreation areas and facilities
    B. Specialized park and recreation areas
    C. Leisure programs that are unique
    D. All of the above

A   27. The number of full time park and recreation professionals in the United States is approximately:
    A. 240,000
    B. 150,000
    C. 100,000
    D. 50,000.

A   28. Benefits based management involves:
    A. Using a medical model for explaining benefits
    B. Developing partnerships
    C. Promoting contracting and privatization
    D. Networking to generate benefit structures

D   29. Personal strategies for park and recreation professional to succeed in the 21st Century include all the following EXCEPT:
    A. Serve others
    B. Become an entrepreneur
    C. Become more flexible
    D. Less formal education

E   30. Within a Youth Development paradigm which of the following is true
    A. Youth are resources to be developed
    B. Programs go to youth
    C. Program build assets
    D. Staff develop relationships
    E. All of the above

CHAPTER 8
Delivery of Leisure Services: State Government

CONCEPT: Goals and functions of state/provincial government in providing leisure experiences reviewed.

See text p. 210	1.	Identify and explain one of the problems and/or challenges facing outdoor recreation managers today?
See text p. 215-216	2.	Discuss the major responsibilities of fish and wildlife personnel in terms of providing leisure opportunities.
See text p. 205-208	3.	Identify and discuss one of the challenges facing state/provincial government in terms of providing leisure opportunities.
See text p. 217-219	4.	Discuss the negative and positive implications of increasing tourism in an area. Is tourism a good thing in all communities?
See text p. 224-225	5.	Should fees and charges be charged and/or increased at state or provincial parks, forests, and fish and wildlife areas? When are fees and charges appropriate? When are they not appropriate?
True	6.	American spend more on domestic travel for pleasure than expenditures by foreign travelers in the United States.
False	7.	Hunting licenses generate more funds annually than fishing licenses.
False	8.	The North Central region of the United States has more state owned land than any other region.
True	9.	Most state/provincial recreation areas would be considered "intermediate" land areas.
False	10.	Technical skills needed for many state/provincial government positions refer to dealing with the public.
False	11.	All fifty states in the United States have state forest systems.
True	12.	States/provinces often employ therapeutic recreation specialists.
True	13.	State/provincial funds are used to support many state fairs.
True	14.	State/provincial governments are turning to more private/public partnerships to meet the increasing demand for tourism development.
True	15.	State/provincial art agencies serve more as an enabler for "the arts" than as a direct service provider.
False	16.	Non-consumptive use of wildlife is decreasing on state/provincial public lands.
True	17.	Fish and wildlife are considered resources of the state/provincial even if the animals are on federal land.
True	18.	As a general rule, recreation facilities in state/provincial forests tend be less developed than counterpart areas in state/provincial parks.
False	19.	The management philosophy employed in state/provincial forests is one of preservation.
True	20.	The first state park in the United States was Yosemite in California.
True	21.	All fifty states in the United States have state park systems.
False	22.	State/provincial government involvement with travel and tourism has decreased in recent years.
True	23.	The importance of state/provincial government in providing recreation facilities and programs is increasing.

C   24. Future challenges for state/provincial governments in terms of recreation include all the following EXCEPT:
    A. Decreasing funding sources
    B. Increasing cutbacks on staff
    C. Lacking technology
    D. Creating partnerships

D   25. Functions of state/provincial government in regards to recreation include:
    A. Legislation
    B. Creation of standards and certificates
    C. Coordination of standards and certifications
    D. All of the above

B   26. The financial resource base of states/provinces includes all the following EXCEPT:
    A. Taxes
    B. Local property taxes
    C. Fees and charges
    A. Endowments and trusts

D   27. Challenge facing managers of state/provincial lands:
    A. Increasing user conflict
    B. Decreasing resource base
    C. People are more involved in the decision making process
    D. All of the above

D   28. A key to success in building a strong state/provincial arts program is:
    A. Involving artists
    B. Seeing the arts as a means to improve a states quality of life index which can be used to recruit new business into the state
    C. Treating support for the art institutions as opportunities to strengthen the state's investment climate.
    D. All of the above

B   29. Which of the following states attracts the most visitors to its state park and recreation areas?
    A. Alaska
    B. California
    C. Florida
    D. New York
    E. Illinois

B   30. Which of the following states leads all states in domestic travel expenditures:
    A. Hawaii
    B. California
    C. Florida
    D. New York
    E. Texas

CHAPTER 9
Delivery of Leisure Services: Federal Government

CONCEPT: An awareness of leisure services delivered by federal government.

See text p. 229-232	1.	Identify and discuss the goals and functions of federal agencies offering services related to leisure and natural resource management
See text p. 231	2.	Identify the key findings and suggestions of the President's Commission on Americans Outdoors. What are the implications?
See text p. 234	3.	What does having a "public servant's orientation" mean in terms of the work of a federal employee?
See text p. 235-259	4.	Pick one major federal agency providing park, recreation, and for cultural services and identify & and discuss its mission and the scope of its services and impact
See text p. 236, 242	5.	Distinguish between a philosophy of conservation and the philosophy of preservation using examples of the mission statements of selected federal agencies
True	6.	There are over 300 federal agencies that provide recreation programs in the United States.
True	7.	Over $2 billion are expended for park and recreation services at the federal level yearly.
True	8.	For information concerning positions with the federal government, one should contact the nearest Federal Job Information Center.
False	9.	Gifford Pinchot is known as the founder of the U.S. National Park Service.
False	10.	Stephen T. Mather is known as the founder of the U.S. Forest Service.
False	11.	The Tennessee Valley Authority is the only federal agency to manage national water resources.
True	12.	The U.S. Forest Service provides more outdoor recreation resources than any other federal agency in the U.S. government
True	13.	The Bureau of Land Management uses principles of multiple use and sustained yield to manage its land holdings.
False	14.	The U.S. National Park Service was established in 1872 with the founding of Yellowstone National Park.
True	15.	The U.S. National Park Service is responsible for managing the United States' wilderness preservation system.
True	16.	The Bureau of Reclamation provides primarily water-based recreation opportunities.
False	17.	The purpose of the Veteran's Administration Recreation programs is to promote a high level of esprit de corps, job proficiency, military effectiveness, and educational attainment.
True	18.	The federal deficit in the United States has severely impacted continued funding of services.
False	19.	The U.S. federal government coordinates outdoor recreation resources through the Bureau of Outdoor Recreation.
True	20.	The U.S. Fish and Wildlife Service is responsible for protecting endangered species, migratory birds, marine mammals and inland sports fisheries.

False   21. The United States attracts small numbers of international tourists, although their economic impact is great on the economy.

True   22. The Land and Water Conservation Fund continues to be a major source of funding for resource acquisition and development, although finds have been cut in recent years.

True   23. The U.S. Forest Service annually attracts nearly 300 million visitors for recreational purposes.

D   24. Which of the following is considered to be a basic function of federal government in relationship to parks, recreation and leisure services?
A. Conservation and resource reclamation
B. Assistance to park and open space programs
C. Recreation programs
D. All of the above are functions

B   25. Of the following, which response best describes the customer orientation of employees in the federal government?
A. Bureaucrats
B. Public servants
C. Quality managers
B. Field monitors

C   26. Which of the following U.S. agencies is responsible for the management of the federal organization with the largest conservation mandate?
A. National Park Service
B. Corps of Engineers
C. U.S. Forest Service
D. Bureau of Land Management

D   27. Which of the following U.S. agencies is responsible for the management of lands within the original public domain?
A. National Park Service
B. Corps of Engineers
C. U.S. Forest Service
D. Bureau of Land Management

A   28. Which of the following U.S. agencies is responsible for the management of the federal organization with the largest preservation mandate?
A. National Park Service
B. Corps of Engineers
C. U.S. Forest Service
D. Bureau of Land Management

E   29. Which of the following is not a part of the National Park Service?
A. National park
B. National preserves
C. National monuments
D. National lakeshores
E. Conservation area reserve

C   30. Which of the following is not a mandate of Parks Canada
A. National historic sites
B. Heritage railway stations
C. National seashore
D. Biosphere reserves

CHAPTER 10
Delivery of Leisure Services: Non-Profit

CONCEPT: Non-profit organizations and leisure services are the key concepts explored in this chapter.

See text p. 263,265	1.	Identify the major non-profit leisure organizations serving your community. Meet with the manager or director of two or more agencies to determine the scope of their operations, including services, funding, and orientation to customers
See text p. 270, 272	2.	Identify and define the sources of revenue available to support non-profit organizations.
See text p. 275, 276	3.	What are the unique characteristics of non-profit organizations serving youth?
See text p. 263-290	4.	Create a plan for a non-profit organization that will meet a newly emerging social need. Prepare a mission statement, list of clients to be served, services, and funding strategies.
See text p. 275	5.	Why are volunteers important to non-profit organizations?
False	6.	Non-profit organizations may divide their assets among members, officers or directors
True	7.	A non-profit organization is a legal entity that promotes in some way a public service orientation.
True	8.	Most non-profit organizations operate with altruistic motives.
True	9.	Most if not all non-profit organizations have some type of fund-raising program in place.
False	10.	Non-profit organizations are prevented by law from selling equipment, clothing, food and other items that generate revenues for operations.
True	11.	Professionals working in non-profit organizations find greater satisfaction in their employment than individuals in comparable positions in the public or commercial sectors.
True	12.	It is estimated that there are more than 400 national organizations providing services to youth.
True	13.	The national 4-H organization is a part of the U.S. Department of Agriculture's cooperative extension program
False	14.	The Boy Scouts of America is the largest youth service organization in the United States.
False	15.	The Camp Fire Girls and Boys program is organized to serve *75* percent females.
True	16.	Many churches operate strong youth programs that promote a philosophy of service, incorporating their beliefs and values.
True	17.	Recreation services form a vital part of many relief and social service organizations.
True	18.	A major challenge among youth service organizations is the establishment of services for younger children, as well as outreach programs,
True	19.	The non-profit sector is by far Americas largest employer.
False	20.	Private benefit non-profit organizations have a broad focus and serve the general welfare of the public.
True	21.	Non-profits take their generic name not from their goals, but from the fact that distributing profits is not one of their goals.

False	22.	A non-profit organization is usually self-governed by a national board that achieve their goals by compliance with normative means rather than an exchange of wages for work
True	23.	Non-profit organizations that promote and provide cultural services are the largest type of this type of organization.
A	24.	Which of the following is NOT a basic orientation that non-profit organizations subscribe to

    A. Financial benefit
    B. Public benefit
    C. Mutual benefit
    D. Private benefit

C	25.	Which youth service organization serves the largest number of youth?

    A. Boy Scouts of America
    B. Boys and Girls Clubs
    C. YMCA of the U.S.A
    D. Junior Achievement

C	26.	Which of the following is a religious-sponsor organization?

    A. Boy Scouts of America
    B Boys and Girls Clubs
    C. YMCA of the U.S.A.
    D. Junior Achievement

D	27.	The number of volunteers working in the non-profit sector in the United States is estimated to be:

    A. 20 million individuals
    B. 40 million individuals
    C. 60 million individuals
    D. 80 million individuals

A	28.	The budgets of national youth serving organizations are substantially supported by

    A. Corporate gifts
    B. Government grants
    C. Foundation grant
    D. Sales revenue

E	29.	Which of the following is not a non-profit association related to leisure?

    A. Fan clubs
    B. Athletic sports
    C. Hobby/avocational
    D. Patriotic
    E. None of the above

C	30.	The best definition of a rank and file member operating within a non-profit organization is:

    A. Originator of the organization
    B. Responsible for the overall management leadership
    C. A member of the organization
    D. Volunteer
    E. None of the above

CHAPTER 11
Delivery of Leisure Services: Commercial

CONCEPT: An awareness of leisure services delivered by commercial organizations is the focus of this area.

See text p. 296-297	1.	Identify and explain the advantages and disadvantages of three major types of business ownerships.
See text p. 294-295, 315	2.	Discuss the types of professional roles and responsibilities of individuals involved in operating commercial leisure service businesses.
See text p. 299	3.	List and describe with examples from your community different types of commercial leisure services.
See text p. 309-311	4.	What is entrepreneurship? Identify and discuss key entrepreneurial skills.
See text p. 299	5.	Locate and define the top ten commercial leisure services in your community. Interview at least two managers or owners to determine the scope and impact of their operations in terms of profit, services, and orientation to customers.
True	6.	Nearly 90 percent of all expenditures for leisure goods and services take place in the commercial sector.
False	7.	Leisure service organizations have as their primary goal, customer satisfaction.
False	8.	A sole proprietorship, although the simplest form of business to establish, is the most costly.
True	9.	Over 80 percent of all businesses are organized as sole proprietorships.
True	10	The number of individuals traveling from the United States abroad has increased in the past decade.
True	11	The travel and tourism industry concerns itself with the movement of people to and from destination areas.
True	12.	Food franchises have become the fastest growing franchises in the United States today.
False	13.	The leisure industry is one market area in which profits have declined in the past decade.
True	14.	One of the fastest growing leisure industries is that known as the casino resort
True	15.	Attendance at thoroughbred harness and greyhound 'acing rank among the top spectator sports in the United States.
False	16.	The percentage of the food dollar spent by each family is declining.
True	17.	Corporations represent 75 percent of all the businesses receipts earned by service type industries..
True	18.	The U.S. Travel Data Center defines travel and tourism as synonymous terms.
True	19.	A tourist is an individual who moves from one location to another primarily for the experience of leisure.
False	20.	Individuals in the United States spend over $100 billion a year on sporting goods.
False	21.	In the past decade the number of foreign visitors traveling for pleasure to the United States has decreased.

False	22.	Most commercial leisure service businesses are organized as corporations.
True	23.	Of all the commercial leisure service businesses in the United States, most can be defined as small businesses.
C	24.	Total ticket sales from lotteries exceeds_____.

24.
A. $10 billion annually
B. $25 billion annually
C. $35 billion annually
D. $50 billion annually

B 25. In the United States there are nearly _____ hotels and motels
A. 40,000
B. 50,000
C. 60,000
D. 70,00

C 26. Borrowing money from another source is known as
A. Equity financing
B. Marginal financing
C. Debt financing
D. None of the above

C 27. When two or more people voluntarily decide to pool their resources and abilities and go into business for profit, it is known as:
A. Sole proprietorship
B. Partnership
C. Corporation
D. S-type corporation

D 28. The principle advantage of a corporation format is:
A. Lack of management conflict
B. Unlimited liability
C. Freedom to act
D. Limited liability

B 29. Of the fastest growing leisure related franchises, which type appears to be the fastest growing:
A. Restaurants
B. Fast foods
C. Sport equipment
D. Learning centers
E. Hotels/motels

B 30. The top leisure industry in terms of market value in *1995* was:
A. McDonald's
B. Walt Disney
C. Eastman Kodak
D. ViacomCarnival
E. Cruise Lines

CHAPTER 12
Delivery of Leisure Services: Therapeutic Recreation

CONCEPT: Therapeutic recreation and inclusive recreation programs are reviewed.

See text p. 330-331	1.	Define both special recreation and therapeutic recreation. What differentiates these two concepts?
See text p. 324	2.	What is an advocate? List two ways you can be an advocate for people with disabilities in your job and community.
See text p. 332-334	3.	Describe the types of therapeutic recreation programs that would be classified as a community or clinical program/setting.
See text p. 337.338	4.	Identify one growing social issue and discuss the role of therapeutic recreation in addressing this social issue. What challenges and opportunities does this social issue create for therapeutic recreation specialists?
See text p. 332-334	5.	Identify one specific settings for therapeutic recreation programs in which you might like to work. Why did you choose this setting? What role does therapeutic recreation play in program and/or treatment in this setting?
True	6.	An adult day care is an example of a community based therapeutic recreation program.
False	7.	The overall purpose of the ADA is to provide suggested quotas to business to increase the number of people with disabilities working in the private sector.
True	8.	A certification test is required to become a CTRS.
True	9.	The right to leisure, self-determination, and quality of life are three broad values advocated by the National Therapeutic Recreation Society.
True	10.	A person who is paralyzed on one half side of their body is referred to a hemiplegia.
True	11.	We are moving to a more participative, preventative model for health care.
True	12.	ATRA advocates recreation as a form of treatment, hence recreation therapy.
False	13.	Legislation related to recreation for persons with disabilities dates back to the 1800s.
True	14.	The American Red Cross played a major role in expanding the use of recreational activities to treat those who sustained various injuries in military combat during World War I.
True	15.	Beyond providing services, CTRSs often take on an additional role of advocating for the rights and needs of their clients in all aspects of their lives.
True	16.	A beeper ball is an example of an assistive technology.
True	17.	One of the most famous and influential psychiatric reformer of the 19th century was Dorothy Dix.
True	18.	In the American colonies individuals who were mentally ill often ended up in almshouse (poor houses).
True	19.	Third party billing is not a reality for many agencies offering therapeutic recreation services.
False	20.	ATRA's membership is made up primarily of individuals involved in community therapeutic recreation.
False	21.	Dorothy Dix was the founder of Special Olympics in the mid 1960's.
False	22.	Because of limited funding there will be a decrease in efforts to mainstream individuals with disabilities into public recreation opportunities.
False	23.	Anorexia affects more males than females.

C   24. The two main barriers to leisure participation for individuals with disabilities include:
- A. Intrinsic and extrinsic
- B. Apathetic and Financial
- C. Environmental and Attitudinal
- D. Communication and Financial

D   25. Therapeutic recreation programs are offered in the following setting(s)
- A. Hospitals
- B. Nursing homes
- C. Public parks and recreation departments
- D. All of the above

B   26. The three components of therapeutic recreation as defined by NTRS include:
- A. Treatment, leisure education and skill development
- B. Therapy, leisure education and recreation participation
- C. Leisure education, skill development, and recreation participation
- D. Therapy, skill development, and recreation participation

C   27. Each of the following are professional therapeutic recreation organizations EXCEPT:
- A. NCTRC
- B. ATRS
- C. JCAHO
- D. None of the above.

D   28. Developments of the late 19th and early 20th centuries that set the stage for the development of specialized services for a variety of people with special needs include all the following EXCEPT:
- A. Health care reform
- B. The emergence of private and public hospital systems
- C. The playground movement
- D. New technology related to adapted equipment

C   29. Paternalistic behaviors toward people with disabilities include all the following EXCEPT:
- A. Head patting
- B. Giving undue or excessive praise
- C. Discriminating against people with disabilities
- D. Providing help when it is not needed

C   30. This law protects people with disabilities and provides comprehensive guidelines banning discrimination:
- A. Social Security Act
- B. Vocational Rehabilitation Act
- C. Americans with Disabilities Act
- D. Architectural Barriers Act

CHAPTER 13
Leisure Programming: Promoting Quality Services

CONCEPT: Strategies and methods for planning, organizing, promoting, implementing and evaluating leisure services with an emphasis on providing quality services.

See text p. 334	1.	Discuss the relationship between quality and value in the creation and distribution of leisure services.
See text p. 344-345	2.	Identify and define five distinct characteristics or dimensions used to evaluate leisure services in terms of quality.
See text p. 345	3.	Anticipatory planning is a key factor in ensuring the success of leisure programs. What does the concept of anticipatory planning refer to, and why is it important in the organization of leisure service programs.
See text p. 350-352	4.	Identify the key behaviors required to promote positive customer relations In leisure service organizations.
See text p. 356-360	5.	Discuss the key factors or variables that must be considered when planning and implementing leisure services.
True	6.	Quality services are those perceived by customers as attaining a level of excellence
True	7.	The value of a service is measured by comparing ones return on one's investment of time and/or money
True	8.	Service should be the primary focus of any leisure service organization.
False	9.	In the delivery of services, quality assurance may take place after the service has been delivered.
False	10.	Leisure services can be stockpiled or warehoused and are under the direct influence of management.
True	11.	The value-added concept involves adding a dimension or element that exceeds the customer's expectation.
True	12.	Customer-oriented professionals operate with a high degree of responsiveness, attentiveness and willingness to help others.
True	13.	Leisure programming involves the creation and distribution of activities, areas and facilities, information and leadership opportunities.
True	14.	Program evaluation refers to the measurement of the effectiveness and efficiency of services.
False	15.	Instructional leadership involves working with individuals, usually in some type of competitive format.
False	16.	Outreach workers help people understand, discover and define their needs and interests and potential.
False	17.	The major function of a host/guide/interpreter is providing people with a learning environment that helps them acquire specific skills.
True	18.	Outdoor recreation activities depend on the natural environment. True
True	19.	Leisure is a product of culture and culture impacts on leisure program needs.
True	20.	One's cohort group or generation will impact directly on their leisure needs.
False	21.	Just-in-Time Programming involves employing only the required effort or investment to produce a program offering.
False	22.	Agile leisure programming infuses concern for innovation with a focus on quality and use of benchmarks to improve program offerings.

False	23.	Total Quality Program Planning promotes the idea that organizations are organic, flexible, and capable of shifting resources to rapidly meet emerging customer needs.

D   24. The evaluation of physical clues in the quality of leisure service programs is related to which dimension?
   A. Tangibility
   B. Reliability
   C. Empathy
   D. Assurance

C   25. The evaluation of caring and individual attention in the quality of leisure service programs is related to which dimension?
   A. Tangibility
   B. Reliability
   C. Empathy
   D. Assurance

D   26. Adding value to leisure services can be accomplished by
   A. Adding unique features
   B. Improving customer/leader interactions
   C. Maintaining orderliness and cleanliness
   D. All of the above

B   27. To promote greater quality in the delivery of leisure services, one should strive to consistently
   A. Group customers according to need
   B. Exceed expectations
   C. Assemble appropriate materials and supplies
   D. Create opportunities for leadership

C   28. The key factor in promoting positive customer relations is as follows:
   A. Anticipate needs
   B. Demonstrate appreciation
   C. Maintain a positive attitude
   D. All of the above

D   29. Which of the following is not a major constraint to leisure participation?
   A. Cost of transportation
   B. Cost of equipment
   C. Lack of transportation
   D. Program design
   E. Admission fees or charges

C   30. Total Quality Program Planning is built on the assumptions of:
   A   C. Edginton and S. Edginton
   B. M. Glancy
   C. W. Edwards Deming
   D. H. Whitmer
   E. None of the above

CHAPTER 14
Professional Career Development

CONCEPT: Understanding how to pursue a professional career in the leisure service area is the focus of this chapter.

See text p. 374	1.	Identify the core elements of the NRPA Professional Code of Ethics.
See text p.371-374	2.	Identify and discuss the four common elements of a profession.
See text p. 371-391	3.	What benefits or services can be derived from participating in professional organizations?
See text p. 384-390	4.	Outline the key elements involved in pursuing a professional career.
See text p. 385-386	5.	What is meant by "career assessment and exploration"?
True	6.	One of a profession's primary requisites is to serve society in some way.
True	7.	Issues such as privacy, privilege, autonomy and other values of leisure dictate a moral position.
True	8.	Professional ethics involve the study and practice of an intellectual endeavor, which leisure service professionals believe must include attitudes and behaviors that add dignity to life.
False	9.	Most leisure philosophies hold that people do not benefit from play and recreation and that it does not contribute to improving quality of life.
True	10.	Involvement in professional organizations creates important opportunities for individuals to network.
False	11.	Pre-professional experiences, which are often part-time or voluntary, have little influence on an individual's long-term professional values.
True	12.	The most important element in developing a professional career is one's education.
False	13.	The half-life of knowledge in the leisure service area is four years.
True	14.	Job opportunities for therapeutic recreation specialists are excellent.
True	15.	The American Association for Leisure and Recreation promotes improvement of the quality of life through the creative and meaningful use of leisure and recreation experiences.
True	16.	The leisure services field has been lethargic in the development and enforcement of a professional code of ethics.
False	17.	The National Therapeutic Recreation Association was founded in recognition of the need for accountability in medical settings where recreation services are provided.
True	18.	The World Leisure and Recreation Association is a nonprofit nongovernmental worldwide agency with consultative status to the United Nations.
False	19.	The National Recreation and Park Association is dedicated to promoting those who have interest in health and safety education, intramurals, aging, fitness research, physical education, athletics, sport, dance, school nursing, outdoor education and recreation.
True	20.	Most professional organizations promote their ideals in such a way as to influence public opinion regarding the worthiness and value of their services.
True	21.	There are over 300 colleges and universities in the U.S. that offer leisure service programs.

False	22.	The most important reason for joining a professional organization is to benefit personally from its services and activities.
False	23.	The uniqueness of the body of knowledge in the leisure field comes from our understanding of human behavior during leisure.
B	24.	Which of the following is not a common element of professions? A. Body of knowledge B. Job performance standards C. Code of ethics D. Public sanction
B	25.	This type of organization provides information and services related to a specific element of the leisure service industry. A. Special interest groups B. Professional associations C. Trade associations D. Futurist groups
A	26.	The job outlook in community-based public recreation can be thought of as A. Average B. Below average C. Above average D. Becoming more desirable
D	27.	Which of the following is a key element in building a professional career? A. Graduate from an accredited university B. Professional experience C. Networking D. All of the above
C	28.	An example of a special interest group in the leisure service area is A. Athletic Business B. Future Focus C. Sierra Club D. National Recreation and Park Association
E	29.	Which of the following is not a goal of a professional organization? A. Advocacy B. Networking C. Research and fact finding D. Communications E. All of the above are a part of the professional organizations
D	30.	The National Recreation and Park Association is an amalgamation of several organizations that merged together in: A. 1865 B. 1906 C. 1954 D. 1965 E. 1993

CHAPTER 15
Leisure and Cultural Diversity

CONCEPT: The pursuit of diversity in leisure service experience and organizations is the focus of this chapter.

See text p. 397-399	1.	Identify common ways that recreation and leisure professionals have engaged in discriminatory behaviors. How can these behaviors be changed?
See text p. 407	2.	Explain how the ADA has impacted leisure services.
See text p. 393-394	3.	In specific terms, identify how a leisure service organization can promote diversity. Be sure to address all levels of the organization.
See text p. 392-418	4.	It is the responsibility of leisure service organizations to embrace and promote diversity? Explain why you believe this.
See text p.408-409	5.	Provide an example of how methods of communication reflect one's cultural background.
True	6.	For discrimination to exist there must also be power.
True	7.	In the year 2020 there will be no true minority population in the U.S.
True	8.	People of color can be racist.
False	9.	Culture relates to the way of life of the dominant social group.
False	10.	According to the ADA it is acceptable to charge extra fees to someone who is deaf to help pay for an interpreter during a recreation program.
False	11.	The ADA was the stimulus for the profession of therapeutic recreation.
False	12.	Inclusion, adaptation, and acceptance are the stages of celebrating and valuing differences.
False	13.	Level of education and religion are examples of primary dimensions of diversity
True	14.	Classism, racism, ageism, ableism, and heterosexism are terms that describe actions and attitudes that indicate that one has a belief that one dimension of diversity is better than another.
True	15.	The underlying premise of primary dimensions of diversity is that they are, for all practical purposes, unchangeable.
True	16.	Integration/inclusion is the most inclusive stage of valuing differences.
False	17.	It is impossible in an agency mission statement to identify diversity or multiculturalism as a primary goal of an agency.
True	18.	Differing communication styles can be the source of staff cultural misunderstandings.
True	19.	Race, ethnicity, age, sexual orientation, physical abilities and qualities, and sex are all examples of primary elements of diversity.
True	20.	An agency committed to diversity has an advantage in recruiting and retaining quality employees.
False	21.	"Surface culture" describes elements of an individual we cannot see.
False	22.	Title IX typically refers to a law related to gay rights.
False	23.	Kwanzaa is a celebration of family, community, and culture aimed at Asian Americans.
A	24.	The trends for the decade of the nineties include:

    A. Increase in multicultural population
    B. Improved environmental conditions
    C. Leisure time increased by half
    D. A decrease in state parks

C 25. A belief that Australia would be a great place to live without any first hand knowledge of living in that country would be an example of a:
A. Culture
B. Ethical stance
C. Prejudice
D. Discriminatory belief

D 26. Leisure settings play an important role in reducing prejudice through:
A. Festivals that highlight a variety of cultures
B. Teaching the value of fair play
C. Classes about other cultures
D. Intimate contact with others in a pleasant environment

B 27. Primary dimensions of diversity include those characteristics that:
A. Are least important in making judgments about others
B. Are not easily changed about one's self
C. Come first to a person after birth
D. Are solely to establish one's social status

A 28. Gender, sexual orientation, age, and race are examples of:
A. Secondary dimensions of diversity
B. Physical traits
C. Isms
D. Primary dimensions of diversity

E 29. Leisure service organizations should look for prejudice in their own organizations in:
A. Promotional information
B. Personnel policies and procedures
C. The design and use of facilities
D. Both a and b
E. All of the above

D 30. White privilege is the phenomenon that describes:
A. The system of privilege for assumed racial superiority
B. The rights of white people
C. The inherent goodness of things that are white
D. None of the above

CHAPTER 16
Future Trends

CONCEPT: The identification of changing trends in leisure including social, health, environment and technology are included in this chapter

See text p. 436-437	1.	Discuss the future of the environment as the trends indicate.
See text p. 441-446	2.	Explain how the changes seen in leisure services as Canada and the U.S. have moved from an industrial to technological to information age.
See text p. 425-427	3.	Explain how changes in family patterns will impact the provision of leisure services.
See text p. 434-435	4.	Identify a contemporary public health problem. How does this issue affect those who provide leisure services? What can be done?
See text p. 420-448	5.	There are many trends that might provide a picture into the future. Which of those trends seem to have the greatest impact on leisure services? In what ways?
False	6.	The population shifts indicate that people are moving toward urban areas.
False	7.	Trends indicate that incidences of teen pregnancy are decreasing.
True	8.	Bird watching, nature hiking, and nature photography are examples of non-consumptive leisure.
False	9.	Eco-vacations include whale watching and trail building.
True	10.	Open enrollment is a trend of the future.
True	11.	Health issues are going to be heavily affected by the increase in the economic differences between "haves" and "have nots."
True	12.	Approximately 75% of youth in the U.S. and Canada are NOT perceived to be "at risk"
False	13.	There is NO relationship between higher levels of education and more discretionary income.
False	14.	As technology increases we are assured of an increase in free time.
True	15.	The nature of work has shifted from production-driven to information-driven.
True	16.	Baby boomers have been enculturated to expect variety in both work and leisure experiences.
False	17.	Cardiovascular disease continues to decline.
False	18.	AIDS is under control and easily treated.
False	19.	User conflicts in outdoor recreation is decreasing.
True	20.	Patterns of behavior that are defined by norms, customs, and rituals of society are known as social roles.
False	21.	Quality of life and balance in one's life are issues that are decreasing in importance.
False	22.	Educationally, it is anticipated that in the future extracurricular activities will receive greater funding.
True	23.	Virtual reality is a type of technology that will allow for interactive and kinesthetic leisure opportunities.
C	24.	Which of the statements found below is most accurate? A. Zero population growth is well established B. Population is one aspect that affects the leisure service profession very little C. The population of the world is still growing at an alarming rate D. Population problems affect mostly those in developing nations

D 25. In the early 1970s a federal law was passed that prohibited discrimination in sport, recreation, and educational opportunities for girls. This law is known as
A. Title 29
B. It 142
C. The gender inequity law
D. Title IX

A 26. Of the social trends is that there is an on-going increase in
A. Numbers of women in the workforce. diversity among people and opportunities for those with disabilities
B. Infant mortality, women in the workplace, and environmental improvements
C. Teen-aged parenthood, opportunities for people with disabilities, and infant mortality
D. Population explosion, white males in the workplace, people who speak multiple languages

C 27. Resource depletion is exemplified by
A. Natural extinction of a species
B. The construction of artificial reefs for fish
C. Draining a wetland to build a shopping mall
D. The greenhouse effect

B. 28. How is the available time to participate in leisure changing?
A. People are taking more extended vacations
B. Leisure time will be available in smaller 'chunks' at varying times
C. Weekends will be the most common time to have leisure
D. Leisure time is disappearing

D 29. An employee is given discretion to organize their work hours around personal schedules and styles. This is known as
A. Flex schedule
B. Total autonomy
C. Job sharing
D. Flex time

A 30. In society people are
A. Becoming older and moving away from urban areas
B. Needing less leisure in their lives
C. Having more children and moving into urban centers
D. Dying earlier from diseases such as AIDS